ARMY TRUCKS
COLORING BOOK

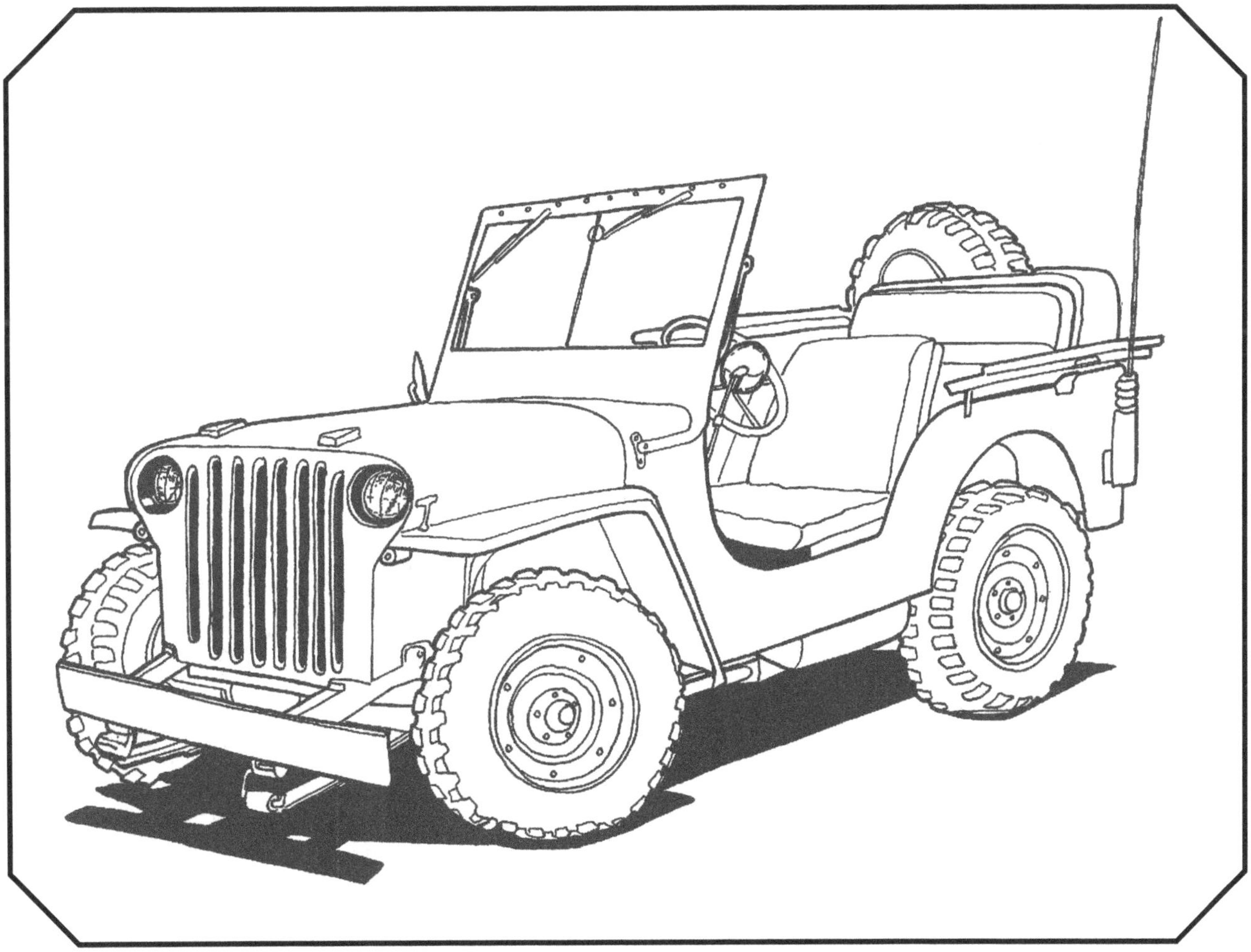

Illustrated by
Kent L. Talley

Illustrations by Kent L. Talley

Published by

R&R Publishing
11805 Sylvester Drive
Oklahoma City, OK 73162-1018
(405) 822-8300
drtalley@drtalley.com
www.drtalley.com

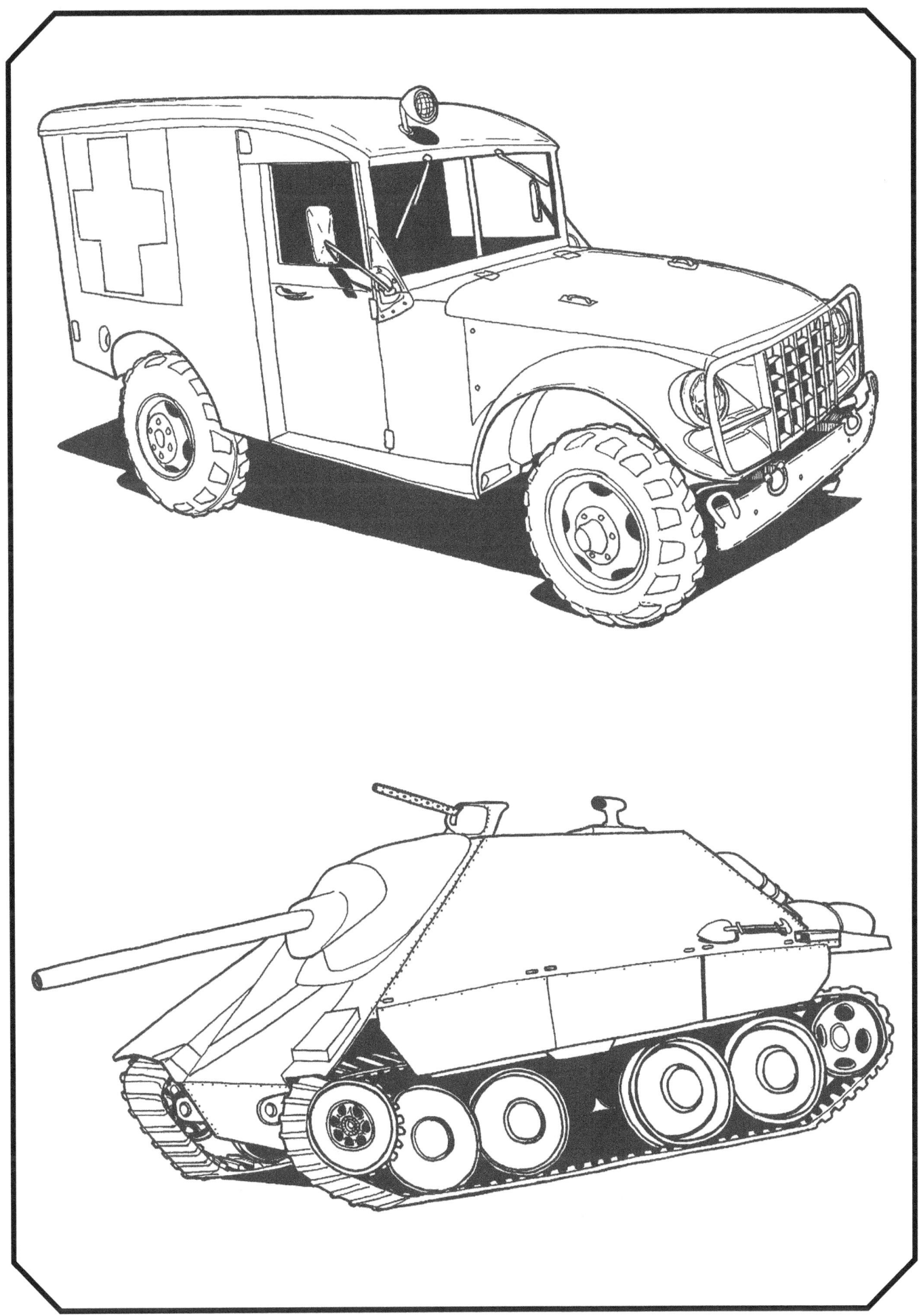

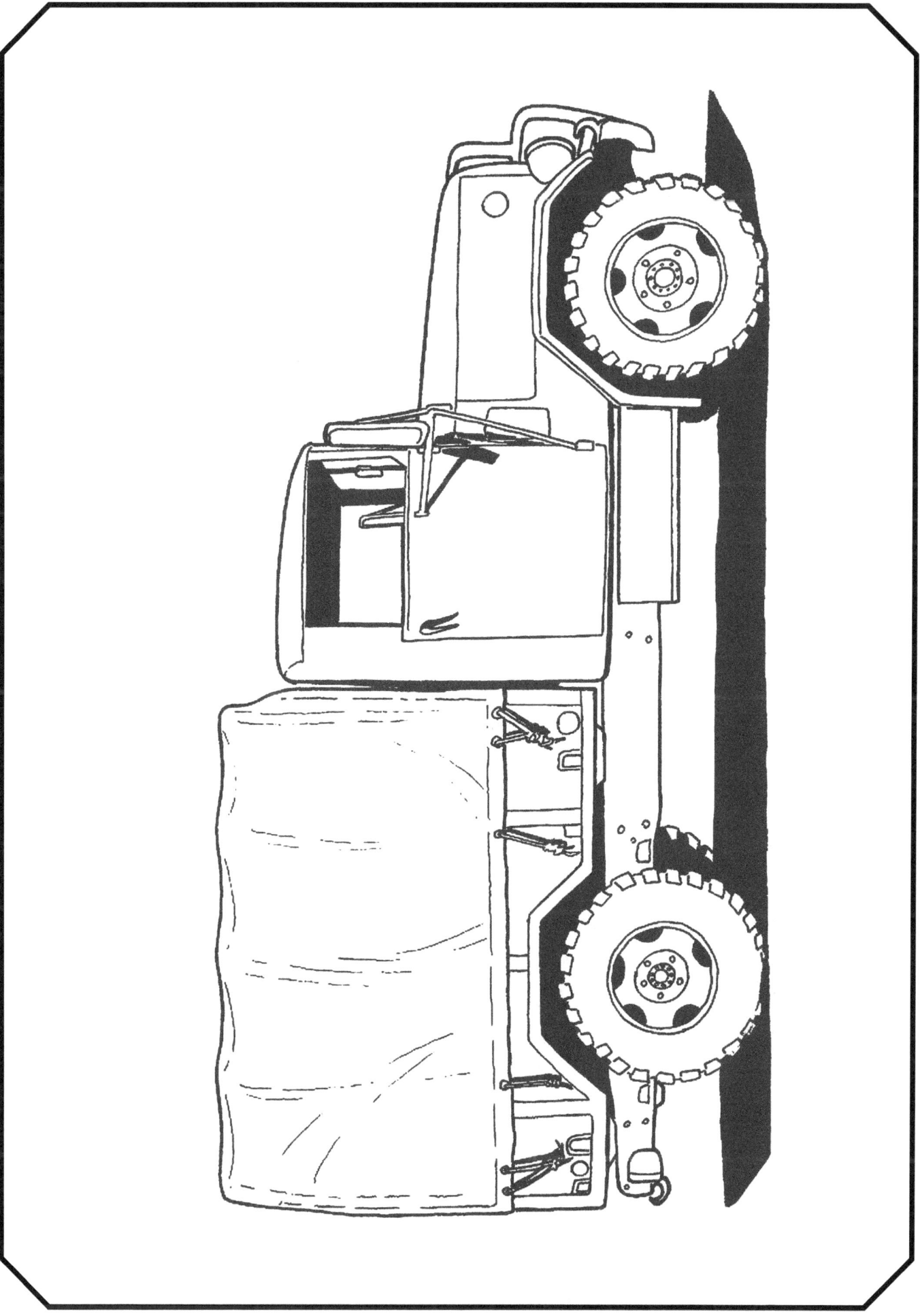

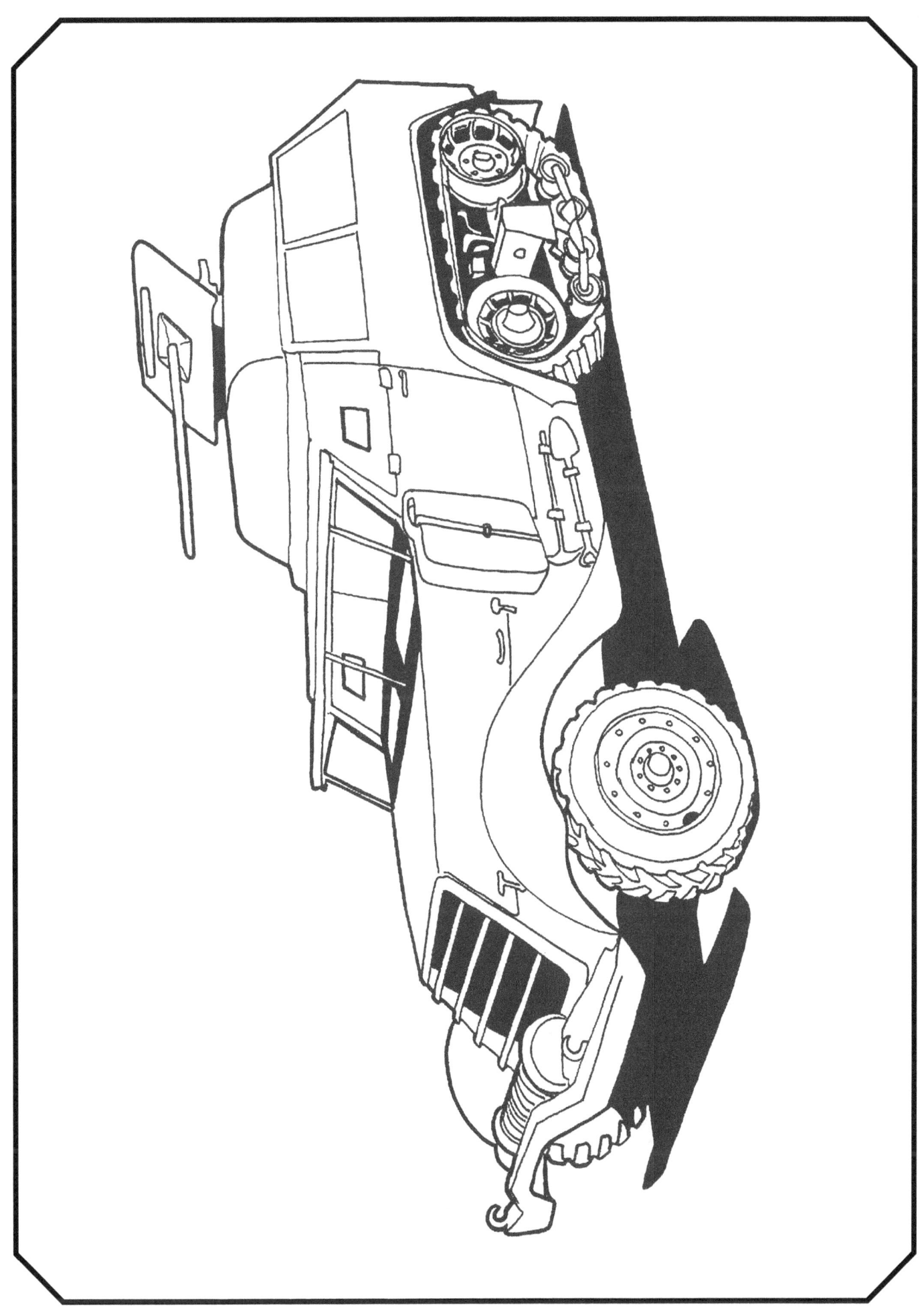

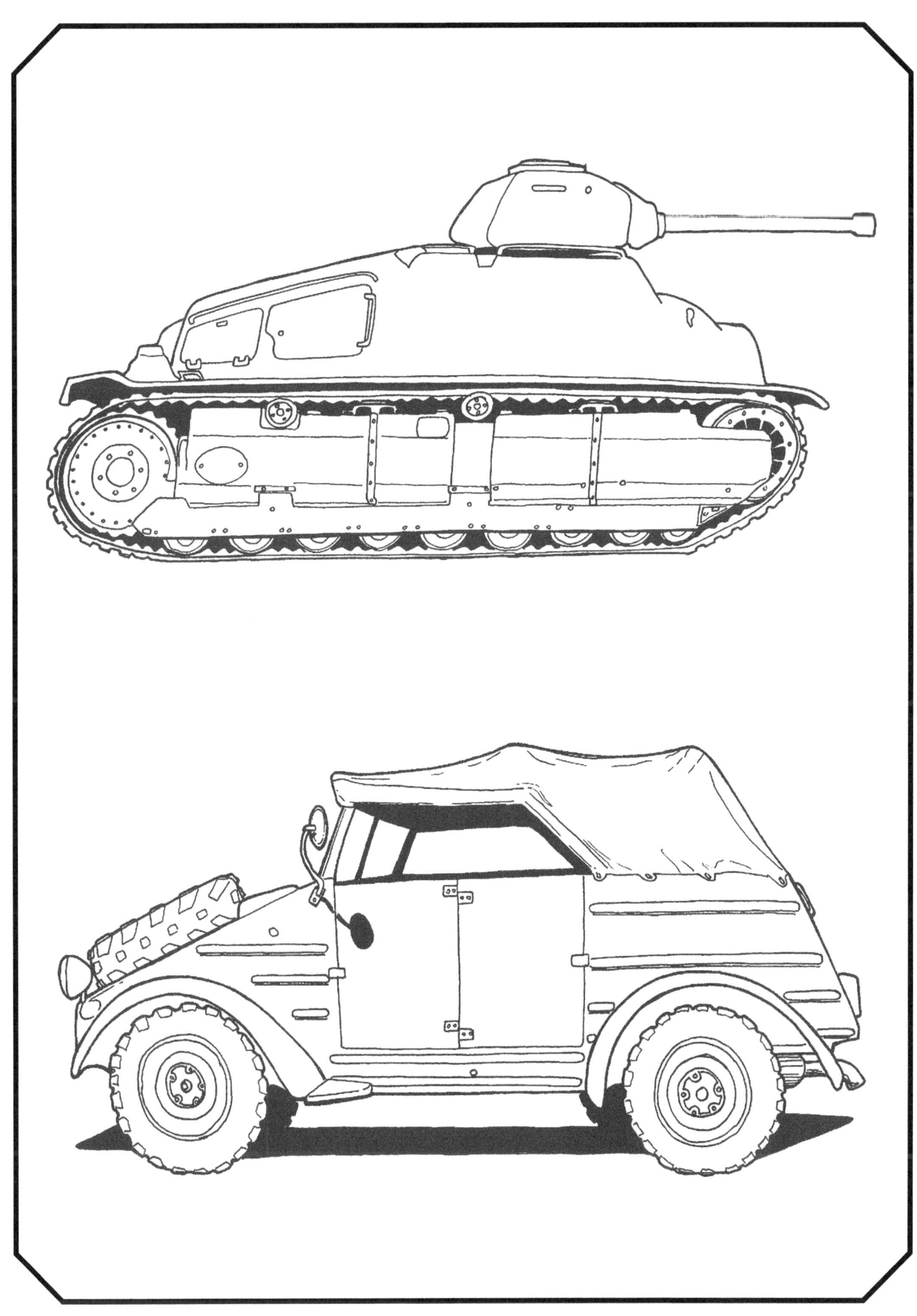

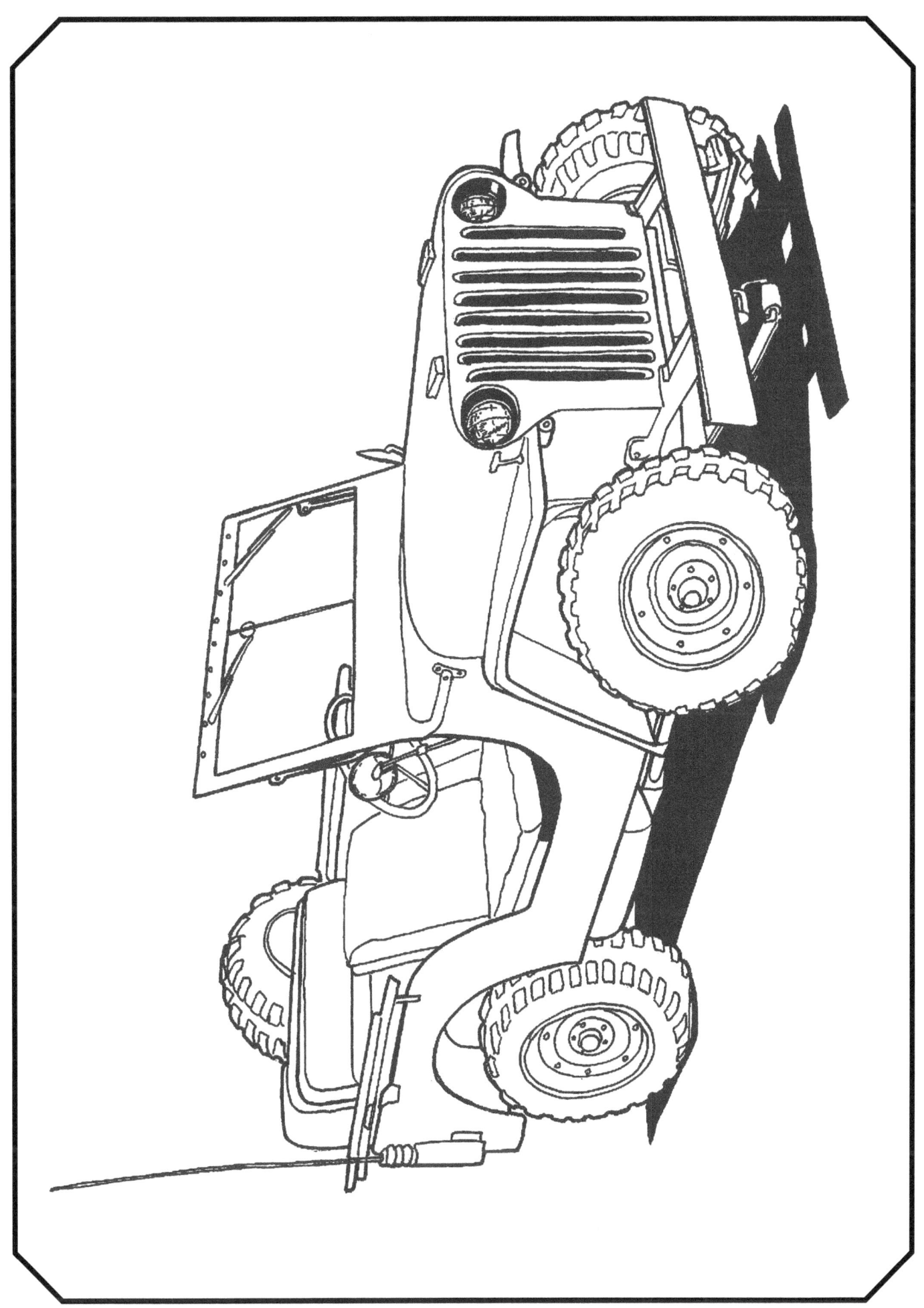

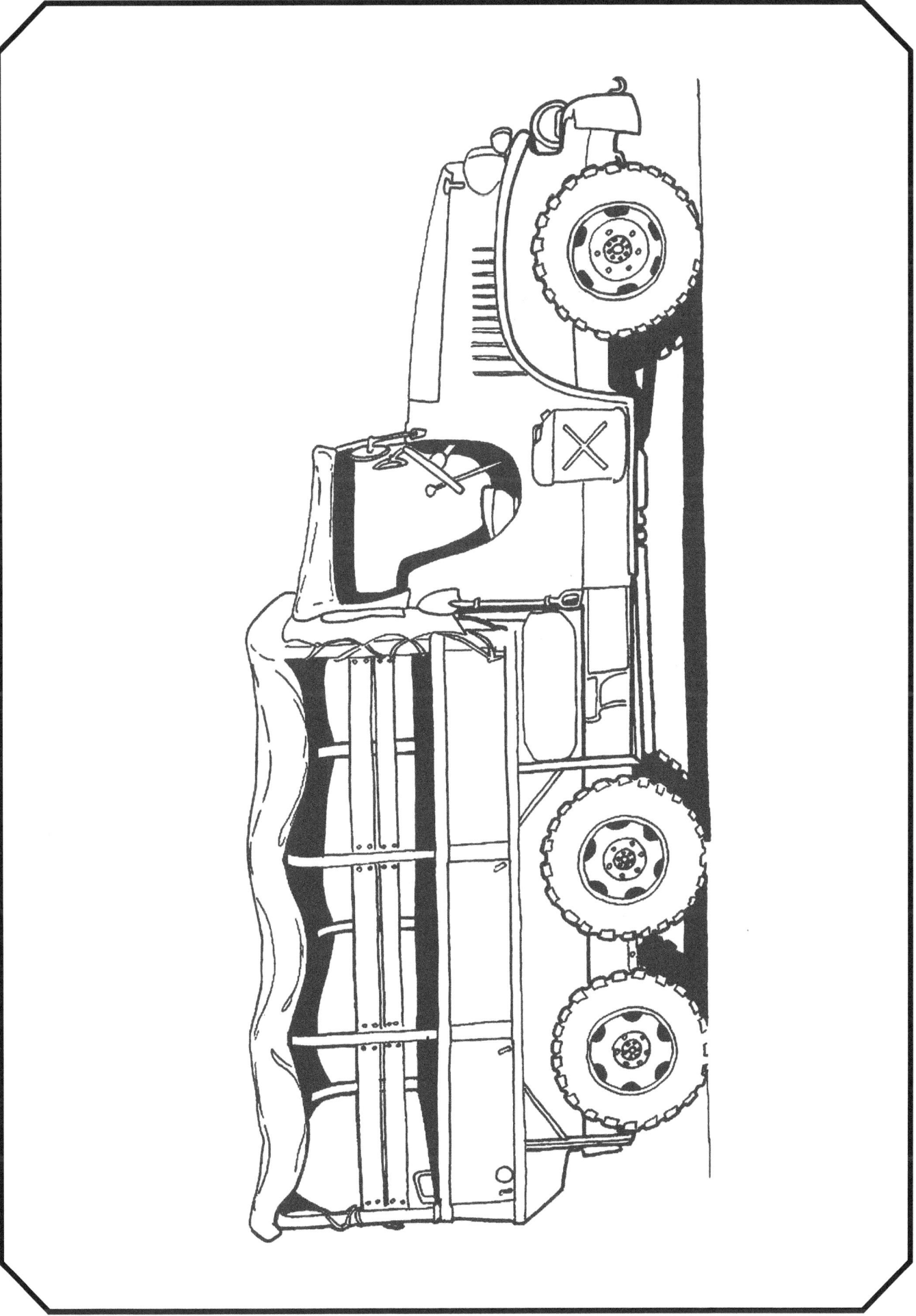

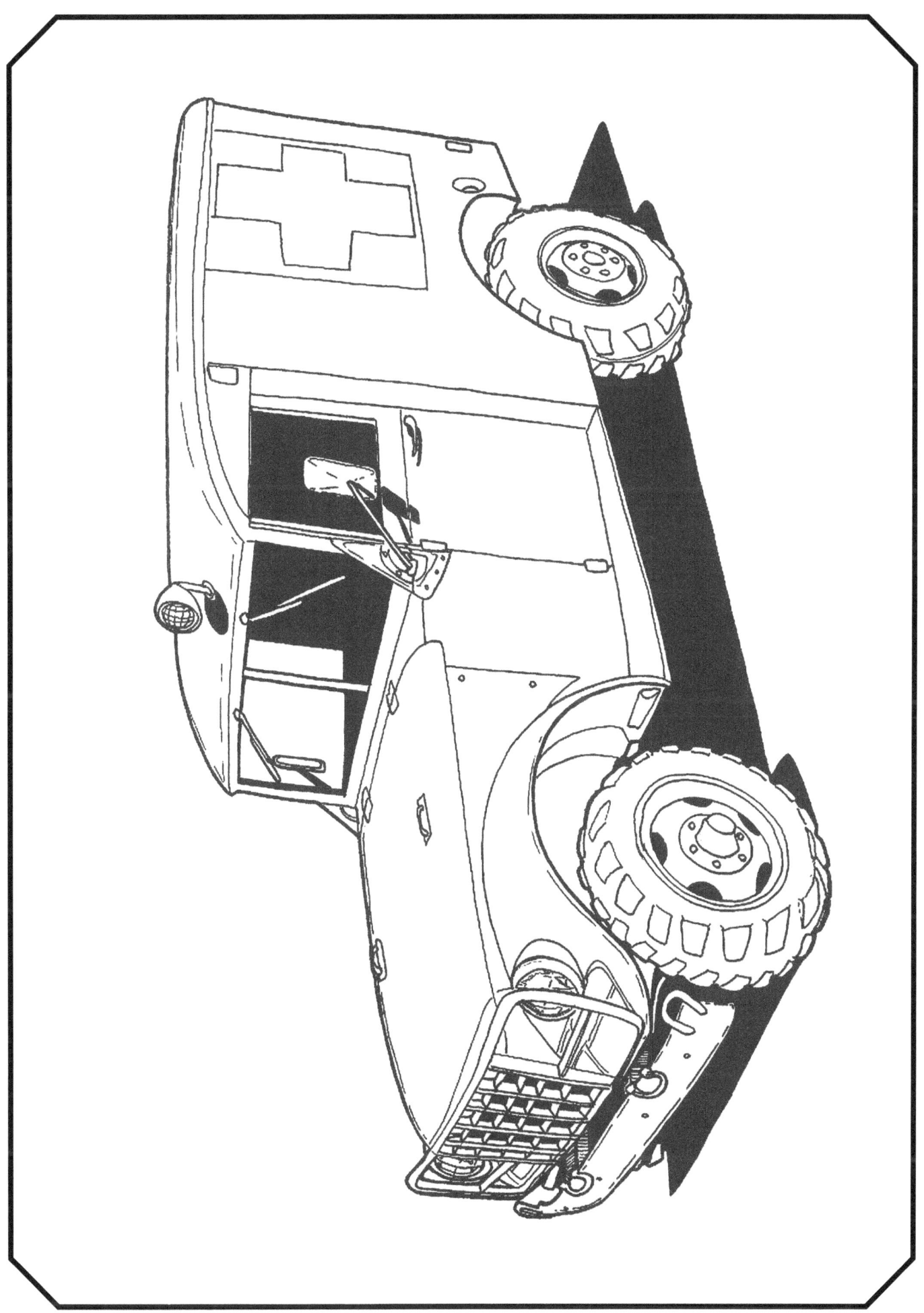

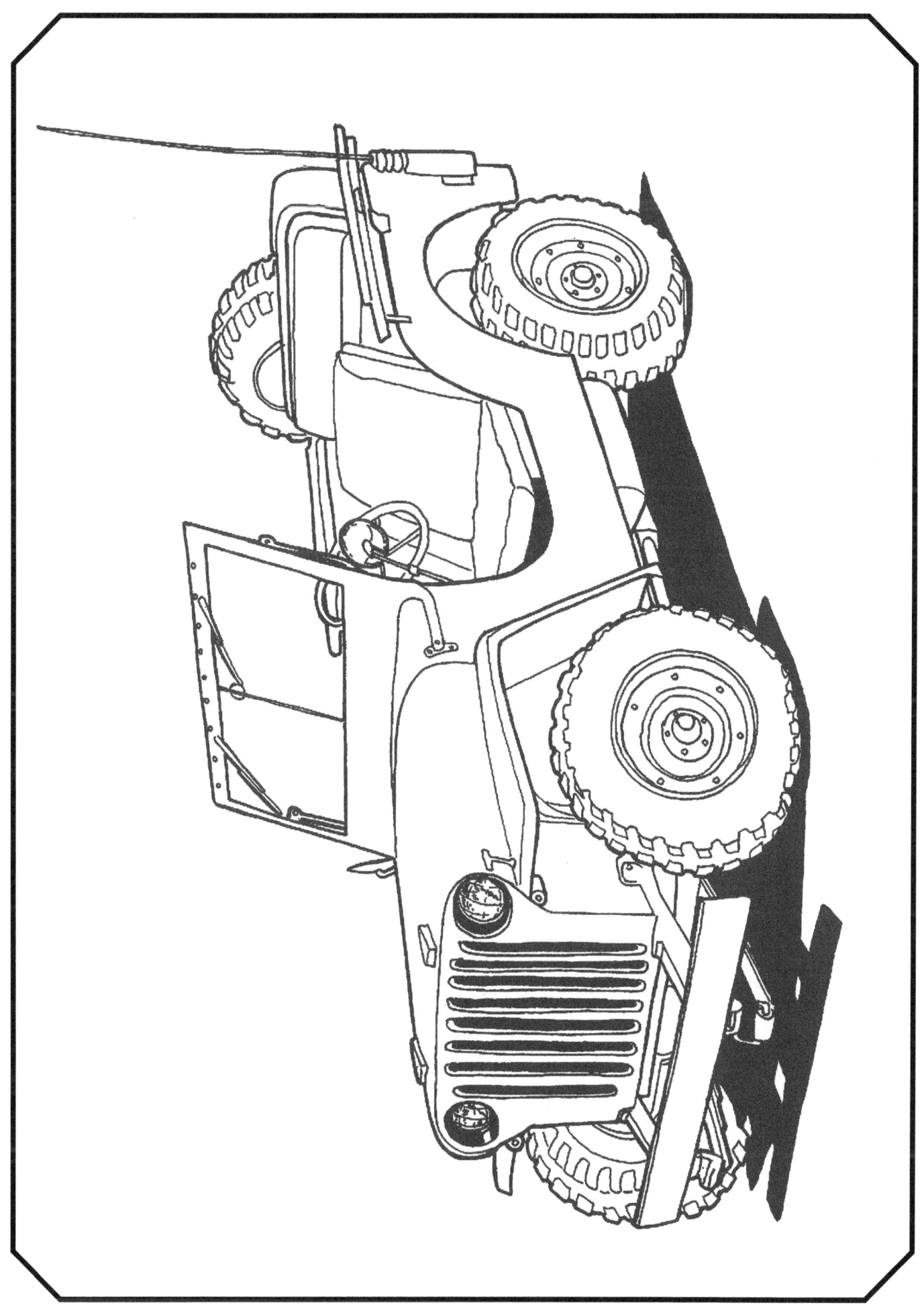

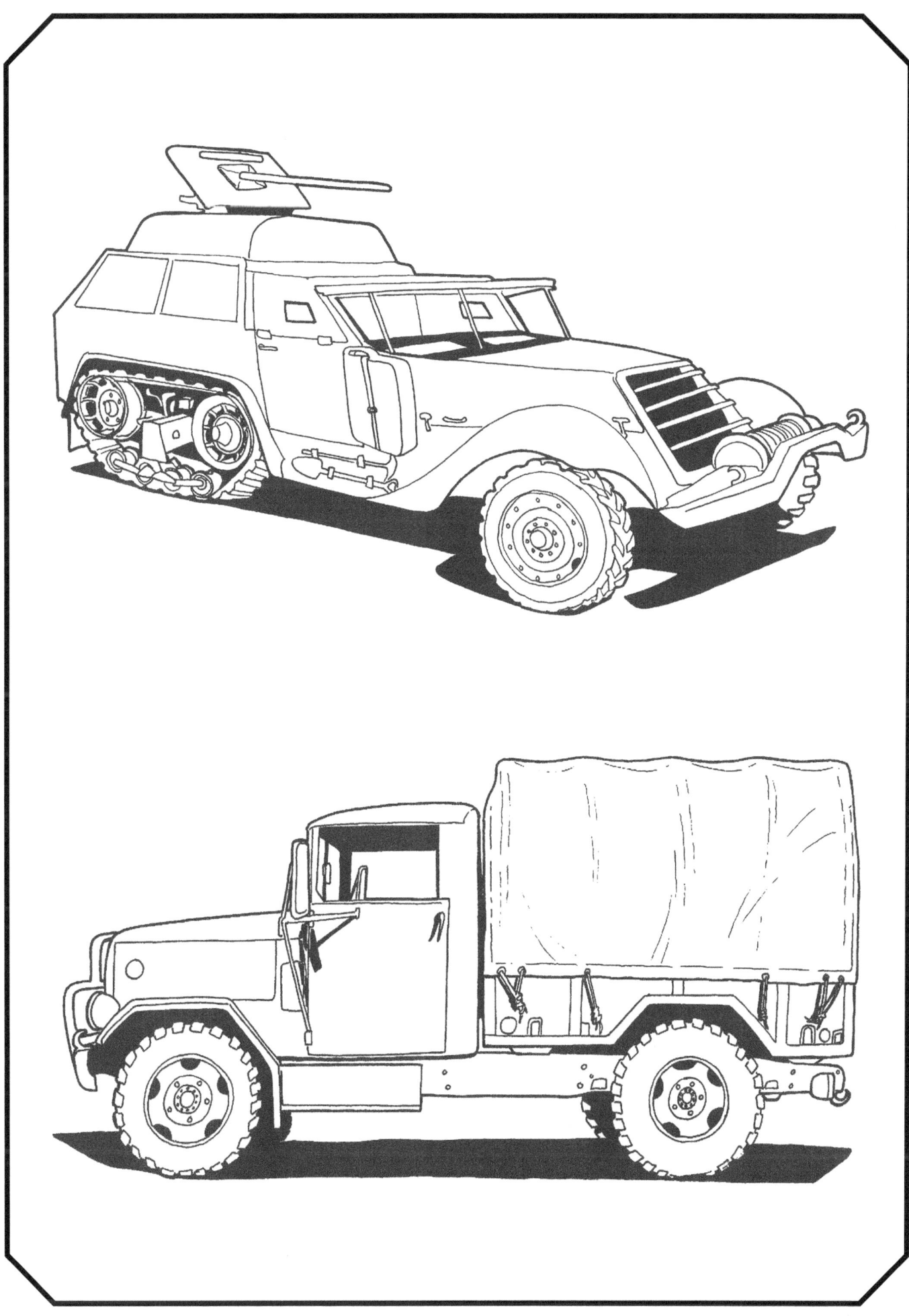

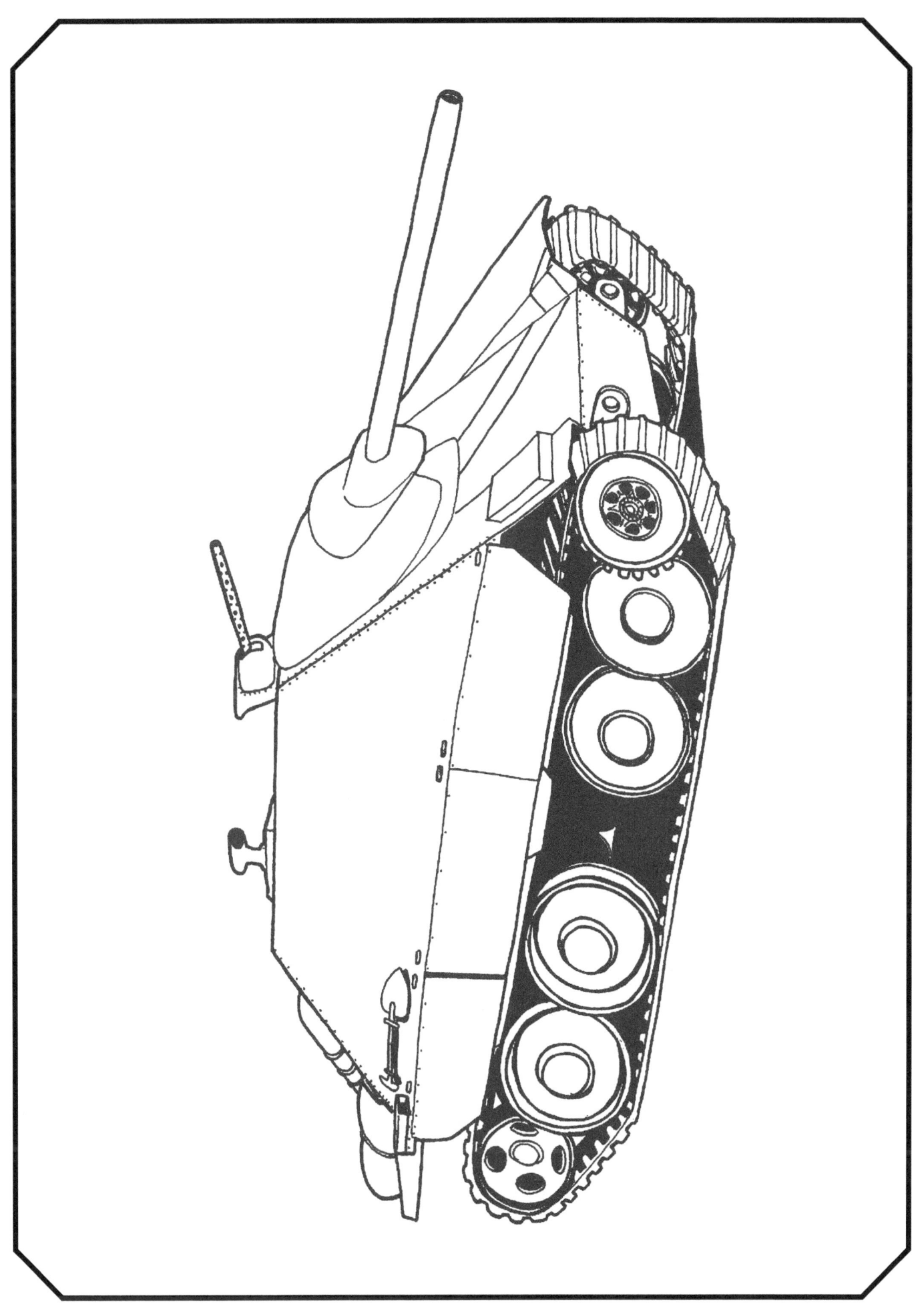

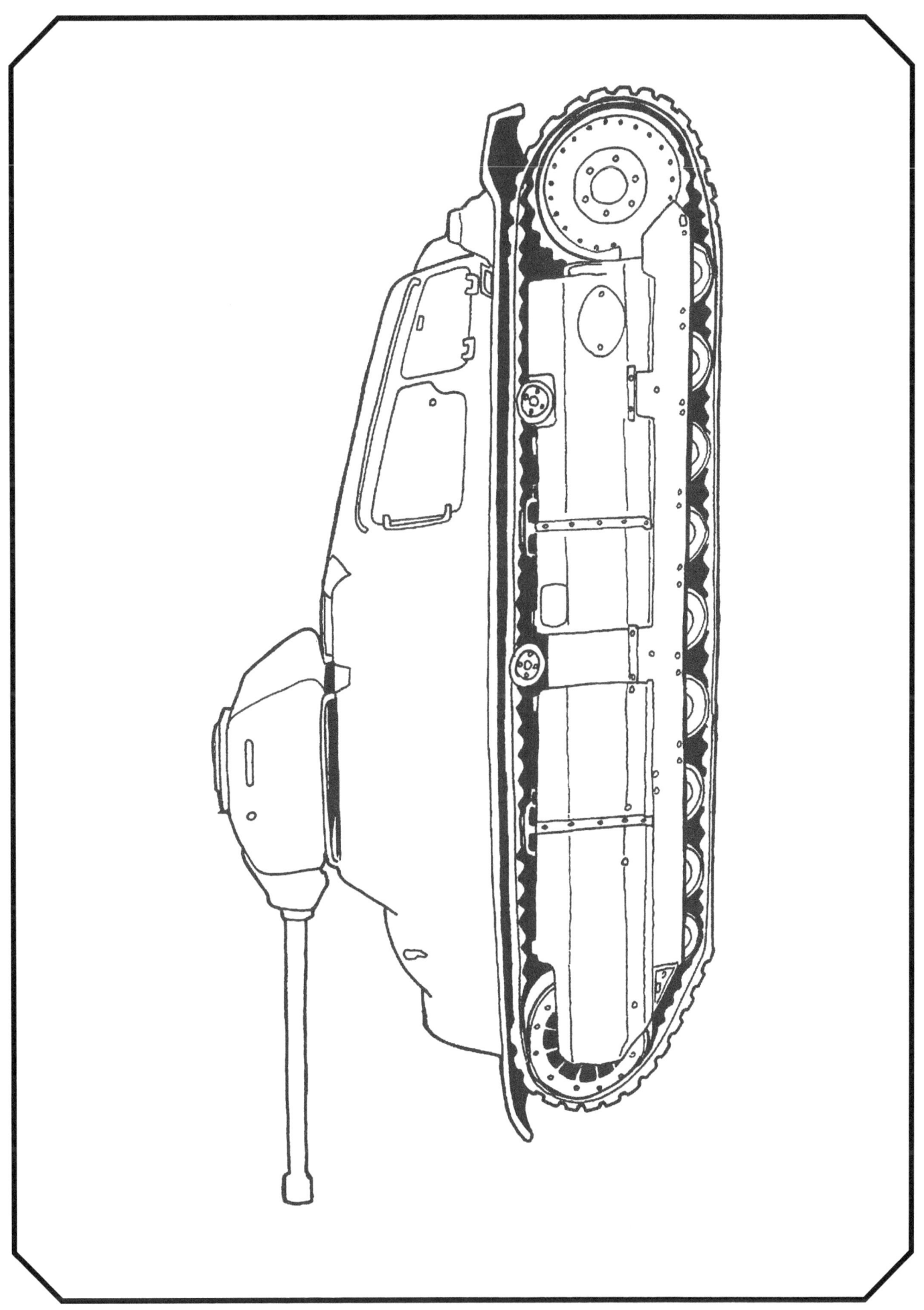

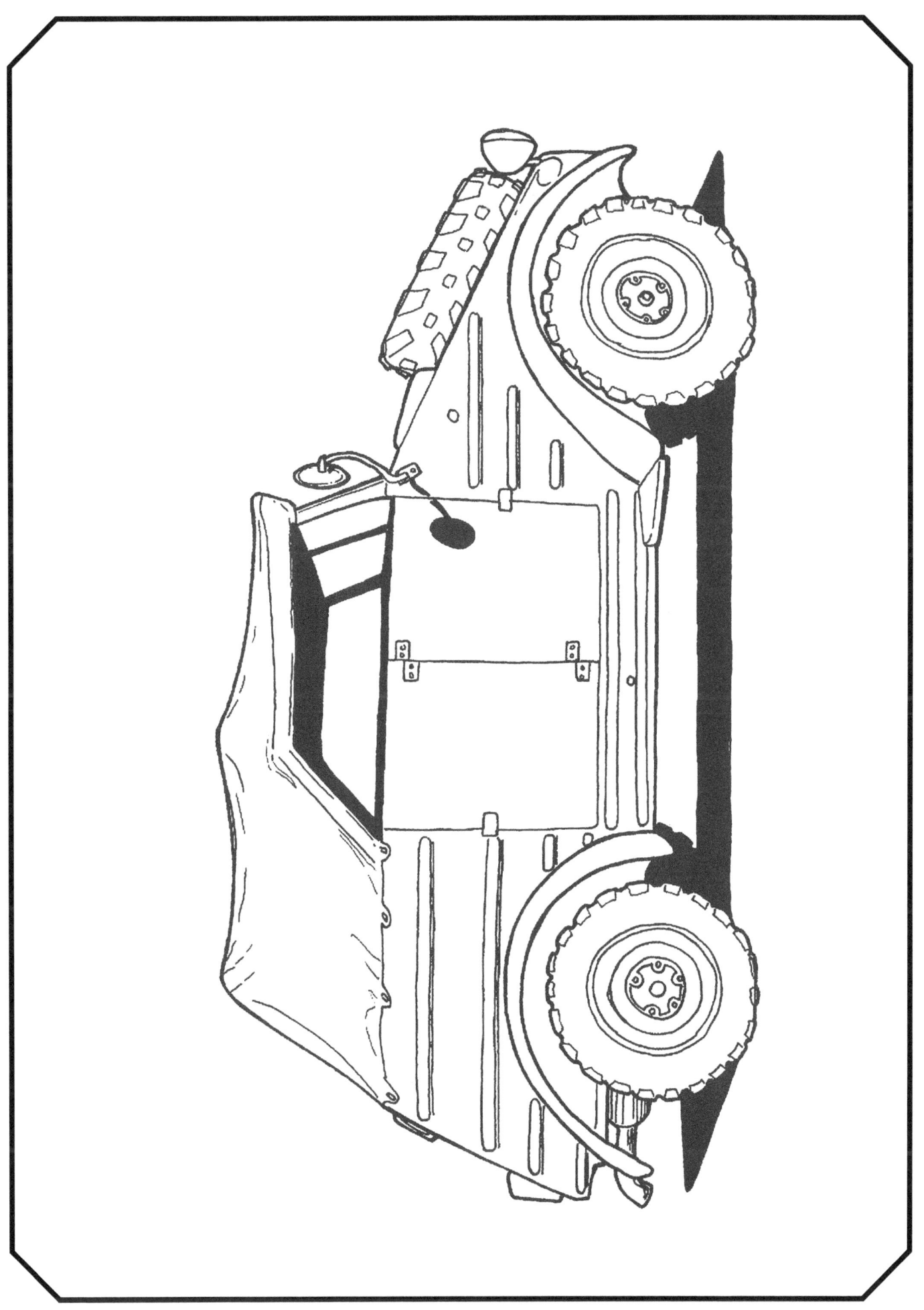

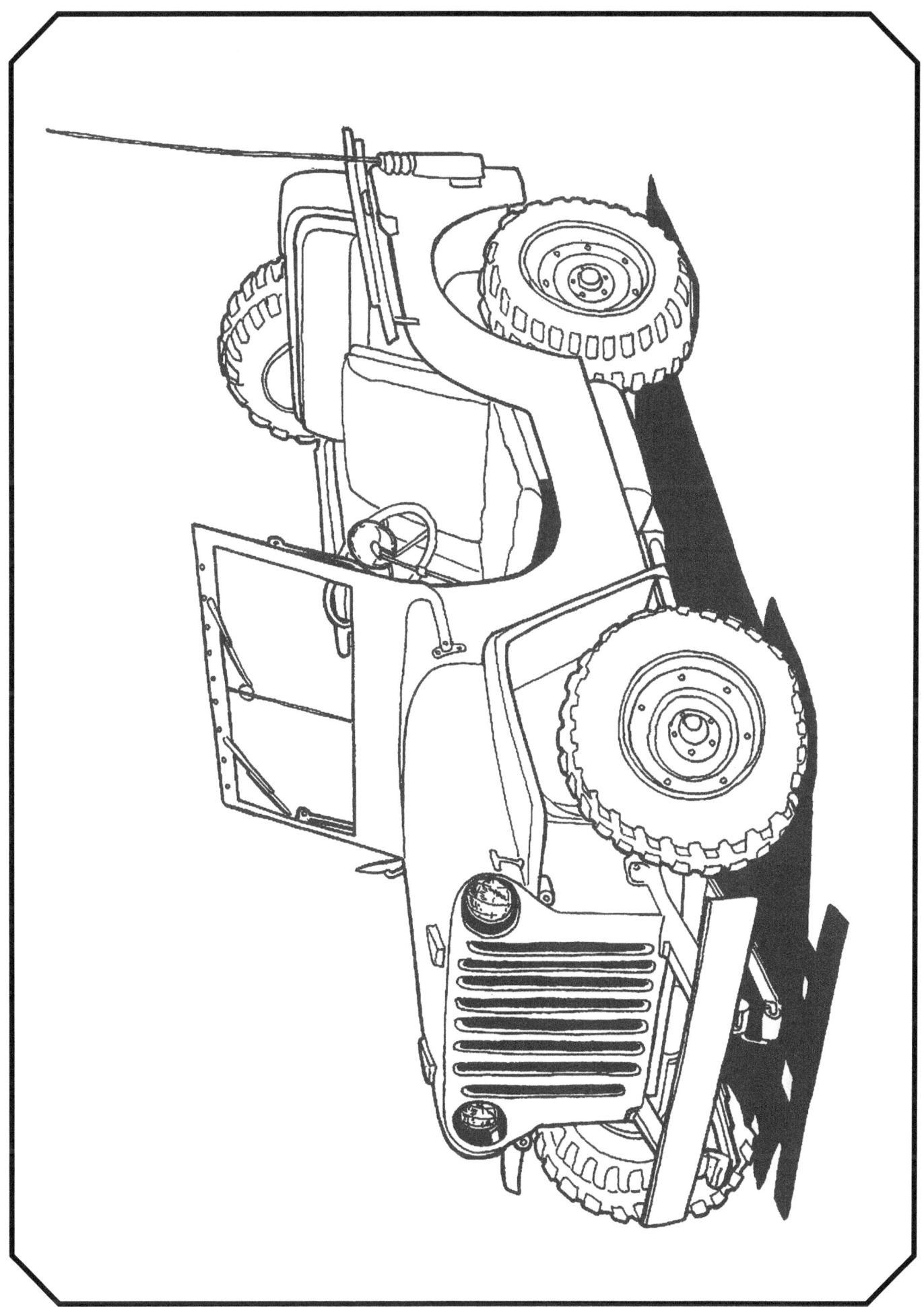

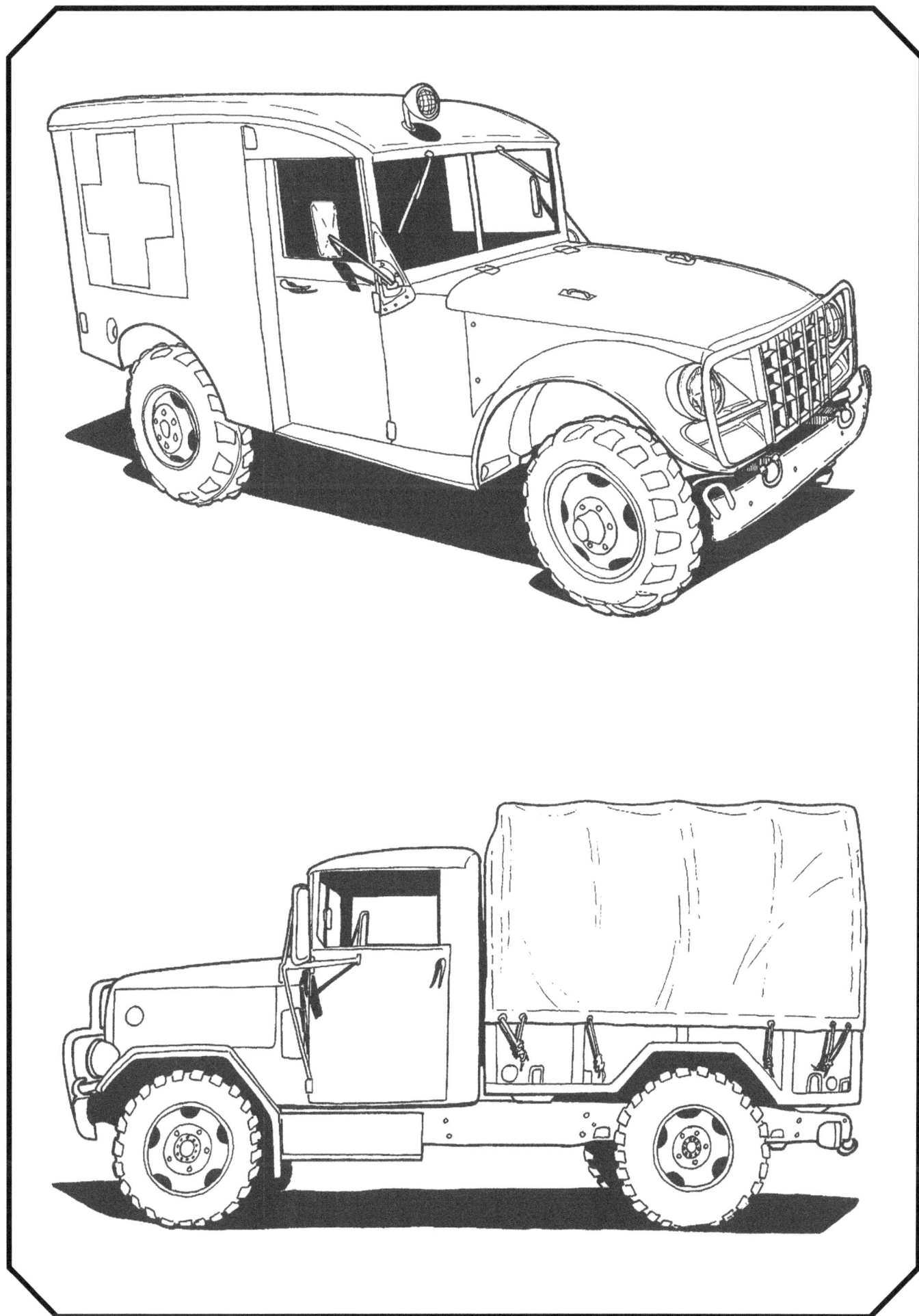

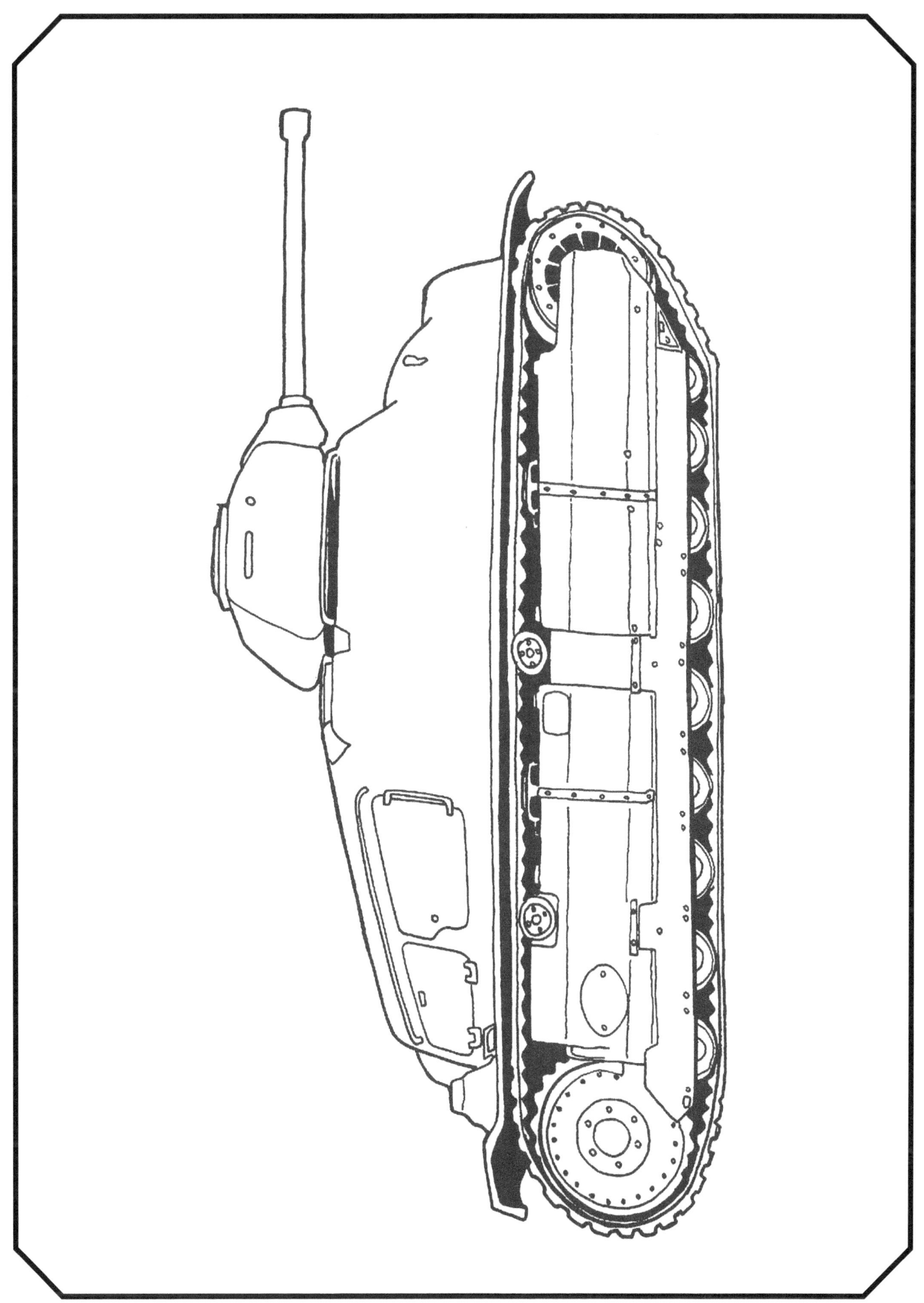

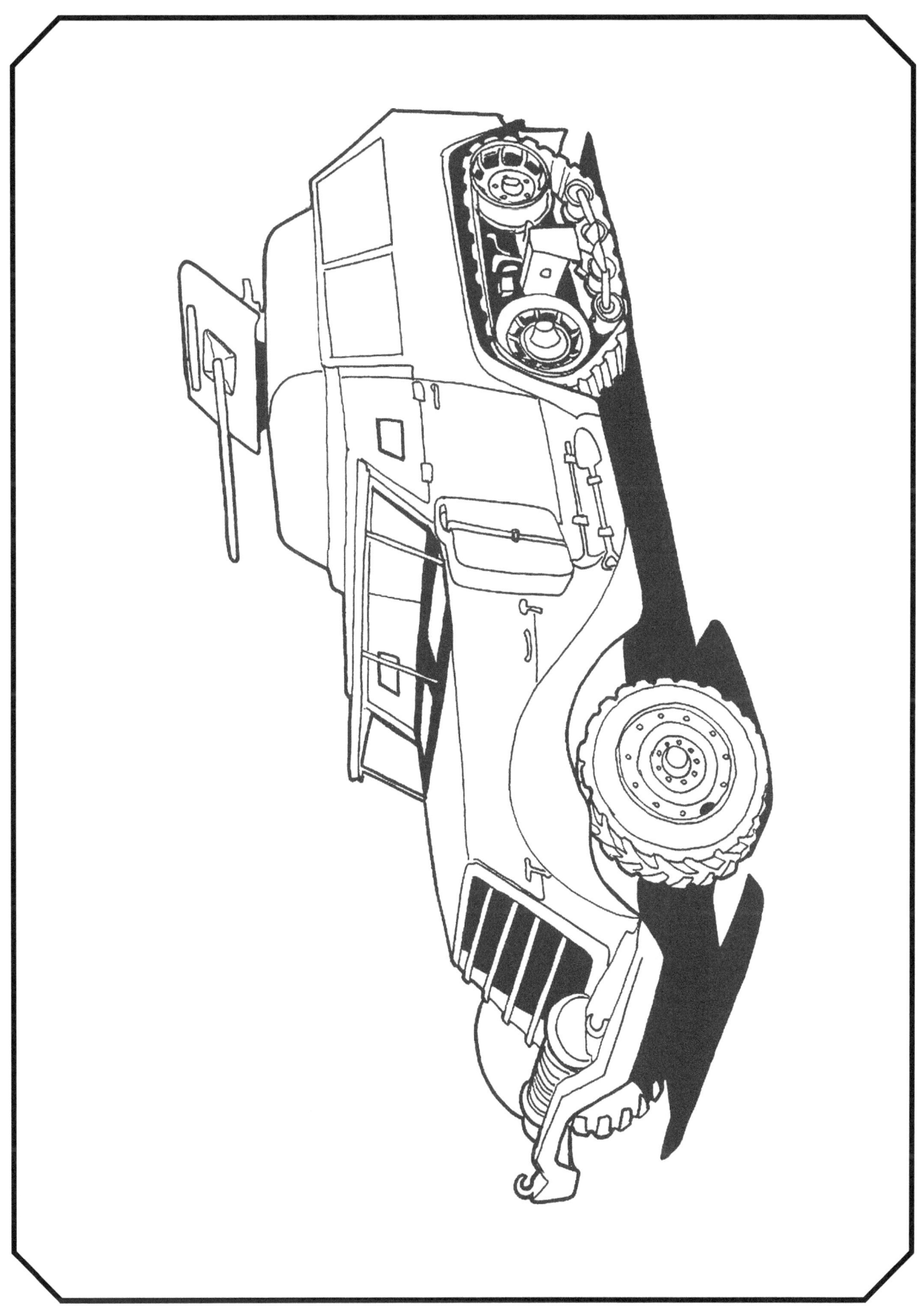

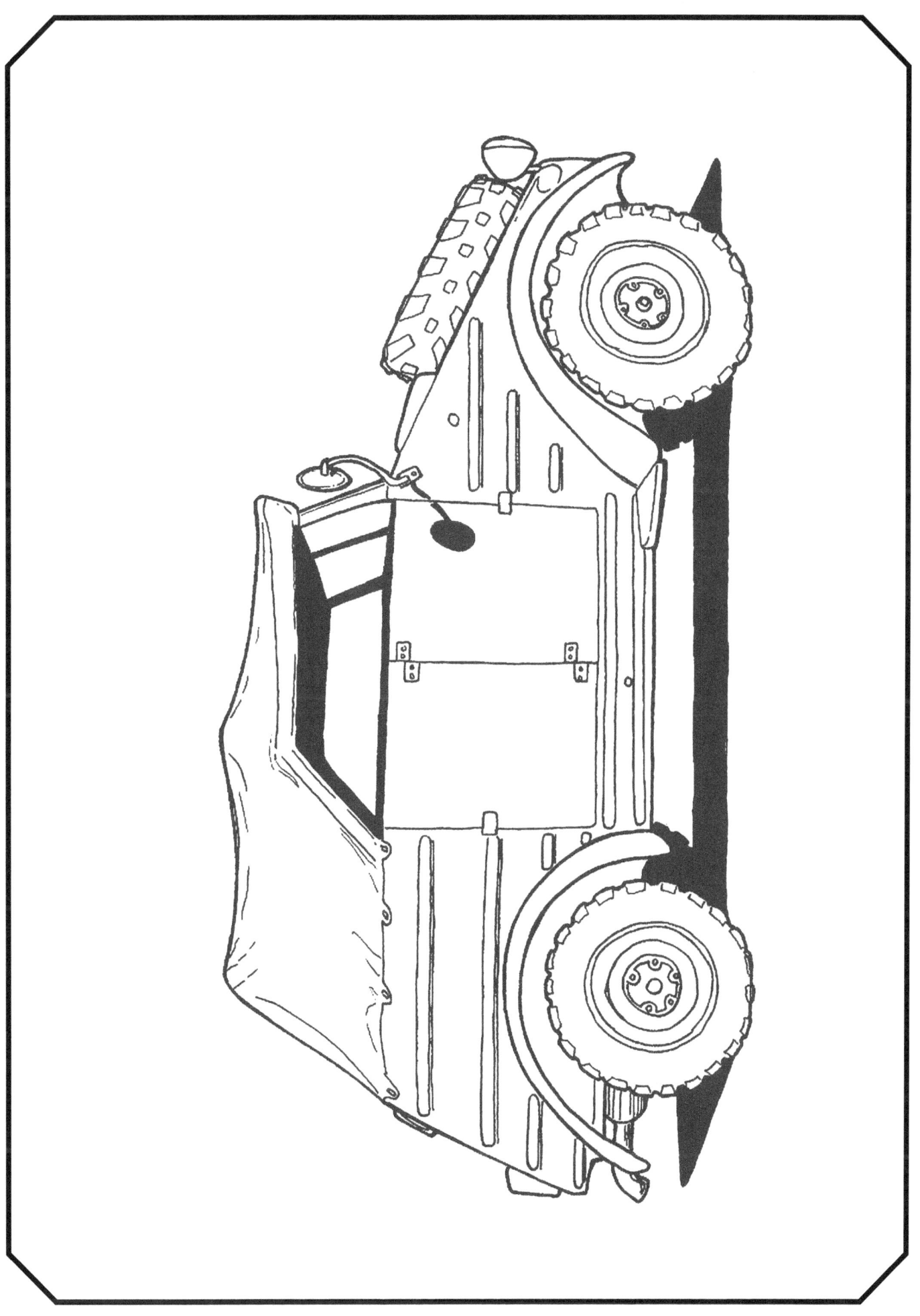

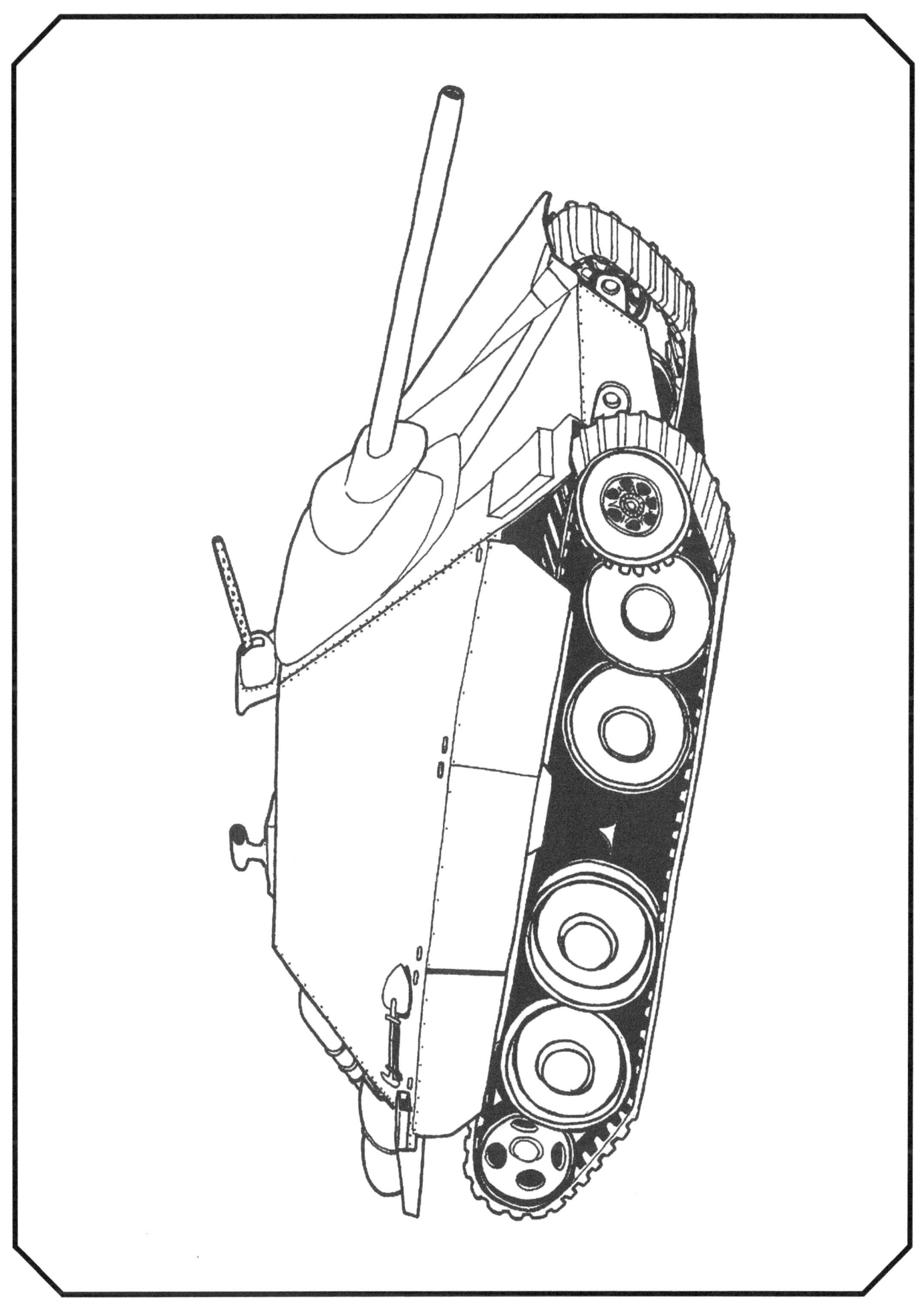

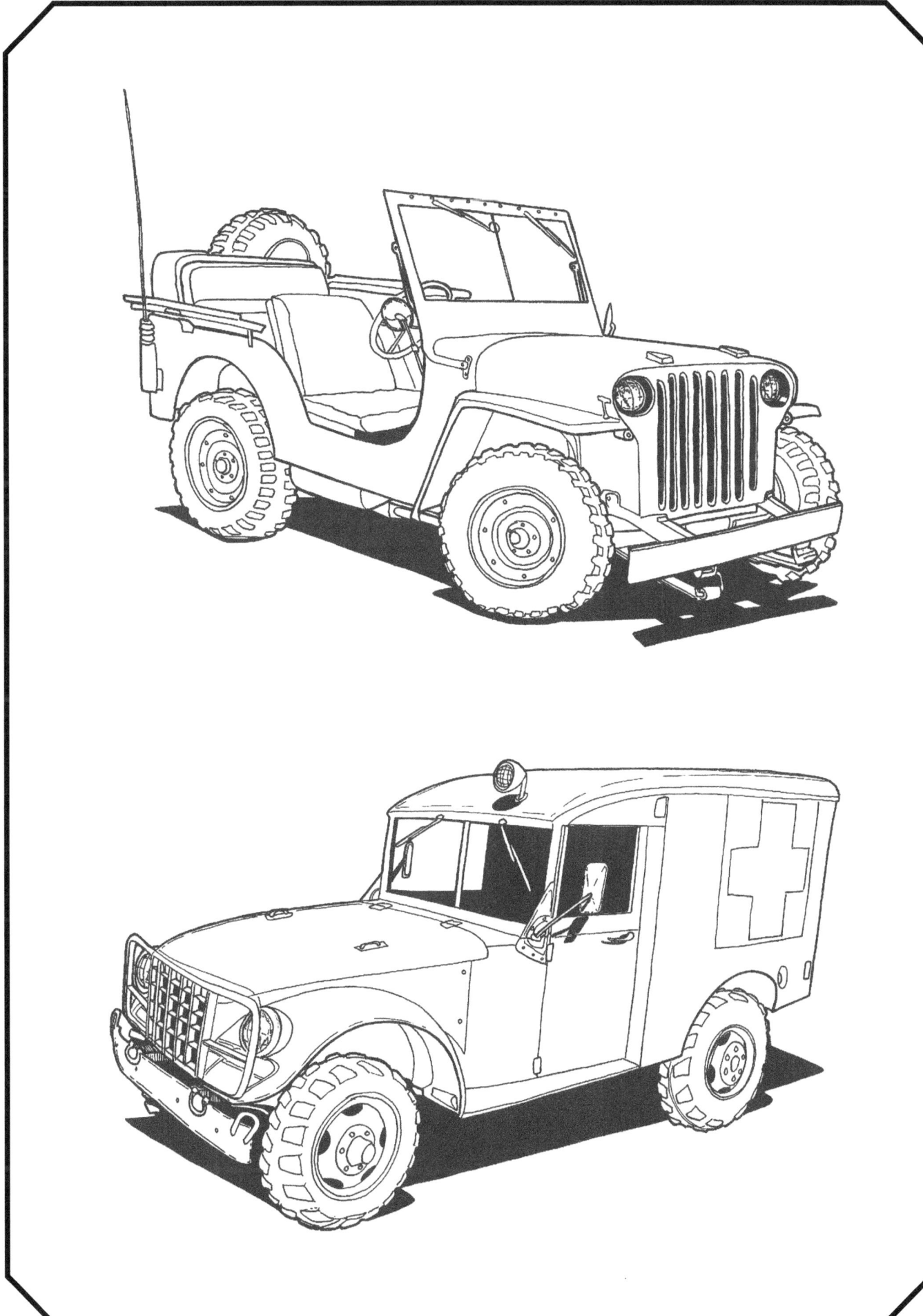

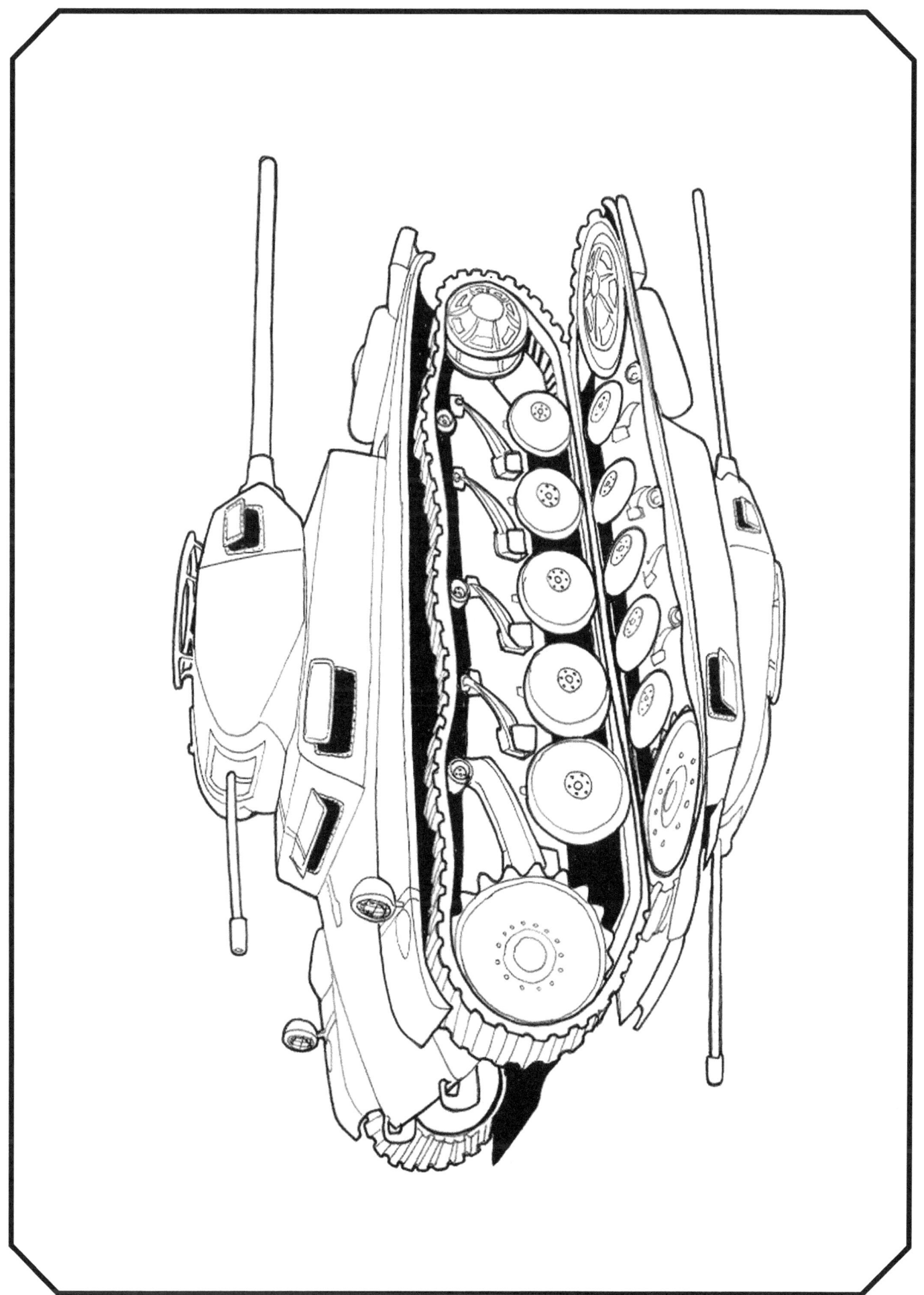

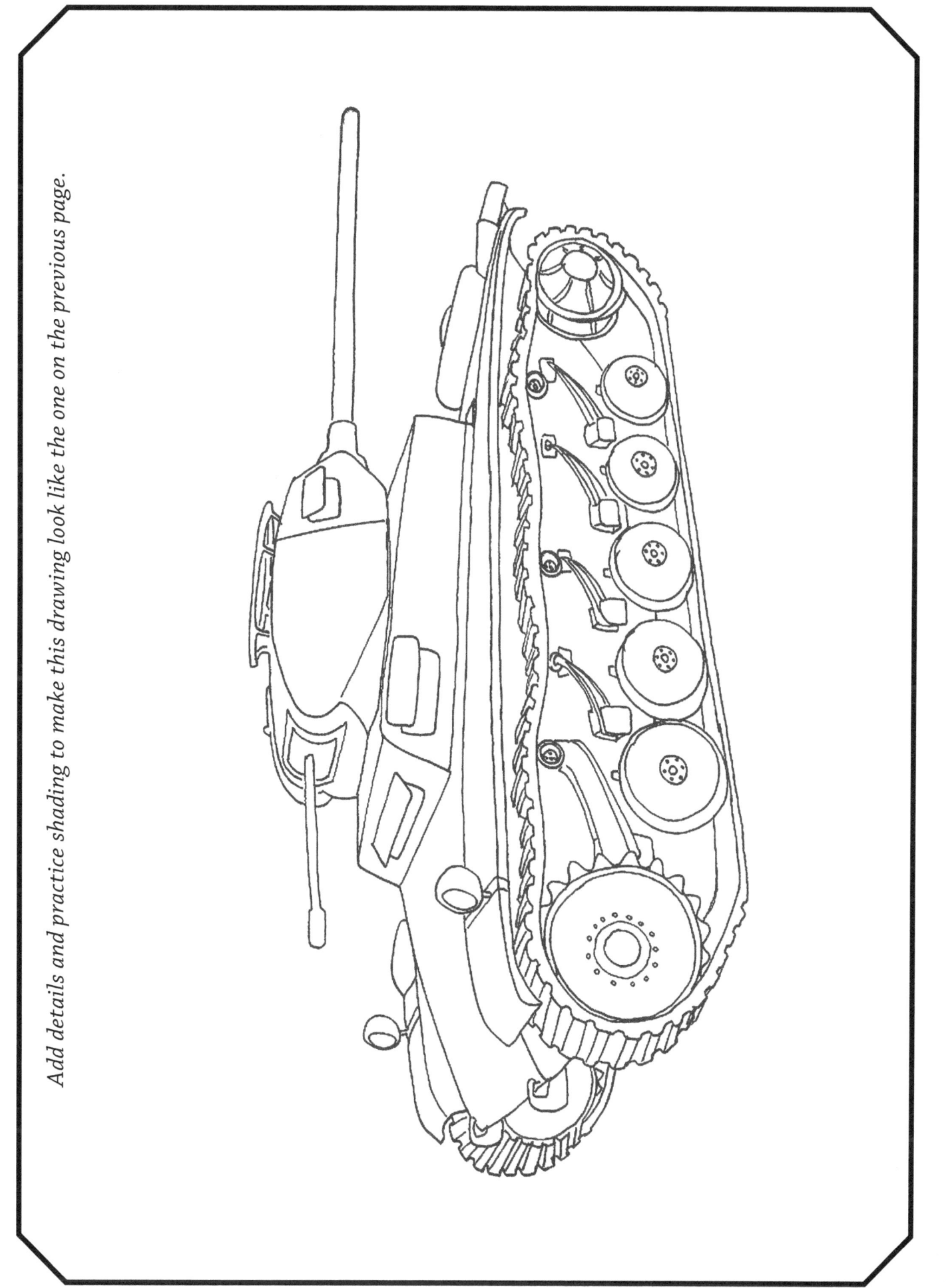

Add details and practice shading to make this drawing look like the one on the previous page.